MORE ALL-AGE TALKS FOR Special SUNDAYS

NICK FAWCETT

kevin mayhew

kevin mayhew

First published in Great Britain in 2015 by Kevin Mayhew Ltd
Buxhall, Stowmarket, Suffolk IP14 3BW
Tel: +44 (0) 1449 737978 Fax: +44 (0) 1449 737834
E-mail: info@kevinmayhewltd.com

www.kevinmayhew.com

9 8 7 6 5 4 3 2 1 0

ISBN 978 1 84867 773 9
Catalogue No. 1501472

Cover design by Rob Mortonson
© Image used under licence from Shutterstock Inc.
Illustrations by Steve English
Typeset by Angela Selfe

Printed and bound in Great Britain

Contents

About the author

Brought up in Southend-in-Sea, Essex, Nick Fawcett trained for the Baptist ministry at Bristol and Oxford, before serving churches in Lancashire and Cheltenham. He subsequently spent three years as a chaplain with the Christian movement Toc H, before focusing on writing and editing, which he continues with today, despite wrestling with myeloma, a currently incurable cancer of the bone marrow. He lives with his wife, Deborah, and two children – Samuel and Kate – in Wellington, Somerset, worshipping, when able, at the local Anglican church. A keen walker, he delights in the beauty of the Somerset and Devon countryside around his home, his numerous books owing much to the inspiration he unfailingly finds there.

Nick has had over 130 books published by Kevin Mayhew. For further details, please refer to our website: www.kevinmayhew.com

Introduction

I will never forget the day at Bristol College when I received the orders of service prior to my first preaching engagement and saw leaping out at me two words: Children's Talk. Clearly this was viewed as an integral part of the service, but what exactly was expected of me, still less how I could deliver it, I had no idea. My experience in talking to children was, to say the least, limited, and there was little I had learned up to that point which had prepared me for the task. Had I but known it, no formal training was to be offered in this field anyway, the learning process essentially consisting of being thrown in at the deep end.

I squirm with embarrassment when I look back on some of the early 'children's talks' I delivered, the content simplistic if not down-right patronising. Numerous congregations must have exercised enormous patience as slowly I developed my technique at their expense. Yet, strangely, the person who taught me more about the art of successful communication than anyone else was not a member of any single congregation, nor one of my college tutors, but an elocutionist I saw for a few brief sessions during my time at Bristol College. His advice consisted of three simple tips:

- always begin by asking a question or using an illustration that involves your audience in what you are saying;
- always end with a simple challenge or question that puts in a nut-shell everything you have been trying to say;
- keep the middle short, simple and to the point.

In every address I have given since then I have kept that advice in mind, not following it slavishly but attempting to apply the essential principles whenever possible. They have stood me in good stead. While I have never considered myself a particularly gifted preacher, still less a natural communicator, the talks I have given throughout my ministry seem generally to have been well received. Why? Partly perhaps because my talks were always short, but most of all, I believe, because listeners could always find something to relate to.

Having said that, every talk is different. The style of a sermon is quite unlike that of a lecture – at least it should be! The style of a wedding address is nothing like that of a funeral oration. Similarly, the style of a children's talk – or family talk, as I prefer to call it – is totally different again. When young people are present in church you are immediately talking to a wide age-range, spanning two, three or even four generations. It is essential not to talk down to children, and equally important that adults get something more from the talk than a pleasant sense of indulgence. This is all the more important if my suspicion is correct that many adults actually prefer listening to a family-type talk than a sermon, the latter often being pitched so far over their heads that their thoughts soon wander to such matters as the state of their Sunday lunch or yesterday's football results!

So what makes a successful family talk? There is no one answer to that, but for me the following are all vital ingredients:

- an element of fun
- appropriate visual aids
- 'audience' participation
- all-age relevance
- brief applications
- thorough preparation
- attractive presentation.

Let me deal with each of these in turn.

Fun

With any audience a little light-heartedness goes a long way towards establishing a rapport. When talking to young people this becomes all the more essential, as there are so many other attractions in our society competing for their time. Too often I have attended services in which the 'talk to the children' is little more than a mini (or not so mini) sermon, and the ineffectiveness of this approach has been eloquently testified to by scarcely suppressed expressions of boredom. Not only do such talks fail to get the message across but, far worse, they effectively drive young people away from our churches.

Visual Aids

My own preference has always been to include some sort of visual aid in a talk, even if this is simply key words stuck to a board. Indeed, words and words games, as you will see, figure prominently throughout this book. It is a fact that what we see stays in our minds far longer than what we simply hear.

Audience Participation

Young people (and many older ones too) like to be involved in a 'learning process' rather than simply being talked to. Games, word-searches, quizzes and other such forms of participation offer an effective way of including the congregation in what you are saying. We need to promote an atmosphere in which people feel part of what is going on.

All-age Relevance

As I have said already, many adults are actually far more receptive to a talk geared towards a younger audience than they are to a sermon. Many also enjoy participation as much as children, if not more so! Even if this were not the case, we owe it to any congregation to ensure that a talk is able both to stimulate and challenge.

Brief Applications

I have always believed that the secret of a successful family talk is to keep the application – the serious bit at the end – as short and simple as possible. Ideally, the message you are looking to put across (and this ought to be one message, not several) should speak for itself through the illustrations and visual aids you use, though some expansion of what this means is usually necessary. Overdo the application and you will pay the price. Which of us hasn't witnessed the sudden glazed looks the moment the 'religious' part of a talk is reached. Whatever you do, don't try and ram the point home; if you haven't made the point through the fun part of your talk, you won't make it afterwards.

Thorough Preparation

There is no getting away from it: talking to young people takes time. There were many occasions during my ministry when I spent longer preparing a single family talk (even one lasting a mere five minutes) than two full-length sermons. In this book I have attempted to do most of the spadework for you through suggesting ideas and ways of presenting these, but to deliver most of the talks you will still need to spend some time in preparation. Don't be put off by this. The effort may occasionally seem out of proportion to the time taken up by the talk during the service, but I believe the results will more than justify it. What you put in, you will get out.

Attractive Presentation

In this sophisticated age, young people as much as adults are used to slick, glossy and professional presentations. While we cannot emulate these, it is important for visual material to be as clear and well presented as possible. Home computers and modern technology make this far easier to achieve than it once was, as well as saving huge amounts of time. While material can be written out by hand (for many of these talks I did just that), I would strongly recommend the use of a PC word-processing package if possible. When it comes to displaying material, my own preference, arrived at after several years of trial and error, was to use a magnetic whiteboard in conjunction with magnetic tape (available through most office stationery suppliers), with the back-up of a second whiteboard (magnetic or otherwise) and sticky tack. If you choose this method, you will need easels for these, as light and portable as possible. A supply of thick coloured marker pens (in washable and permanent ink) is a must for many talks, as is a copious supply of thin card and/or paper. Many of the talks nowadays could be delivered using an overhead projector and screen if this is preferred to board and easel. Adapt to your available resources. On a purely practical note, make use of a radio microphone if this is available. Family talks often involve a degree of movement, and it is all too easy to stray from a standing microphone so that you become inaudible, or, worse still, to trip headlong over the wires of a halterneck model! (The younger members of the congregation will delight in this, but for you it can prove embarrassing and even dangerous.) Each talk in this collection is set out according to a basic framework:

- a suggested Bible passage which should normally be read publicly prior to the talk
- a statement of the aim of the talk
- details of preparation needed beforehand
- the talk itself.

This last section includes instructions relating, for example, to the use of illustrations, together with a suggested application of the talk. The talks will work best if, having read and digested these paragraphs, you present them in your own words. This is particularly true where the congregation is invited to respond, and developing and incorporating their ideas and answers into the talk will require a measure of ad-libbing on your part.

Each of the talks in this booklet was used in public worship during my time in the ministry. No doubt many are flawed in places and could be considerably improved – I do not offer them as examples of how it should be done, but rather as a resource which may be of help to you. Of all the comments received during my ministry, few have gratified me more than those when young people have referred in conversation to talks I delivered three, four, even five years back. Whether they remembered the point I had been making I cannot say, but, whatever else, they clearly enjoyed being in church and carried away positive associations of their time there. That in itself was always sufficient motivation to spend further time and energy devoted to getting the message across.

Nick Fawcett

New Year

A New Chapter

Reading   Psalm 116

Aim   To recall God's faithfulness across the years, and so to look forward to the future in hope and confidence.

Preparation   No special preparation is needed for this talk.

Talk   Tell the congregation that you want to think about stories, specifically about autobiographies written by celebrities past and present. Ask who wrote the following (you may wish to add other more recent titles or personal favourites to the list):

What You See Is What You Get: My Autobiography	Sir Alan Sugar
Taken on Trust	Terry Waite
Humble Pie	Gordon Ramsey
Steve Redgrave: A Golden Age	Steve Redgrave
Behind the White Ball	Jimmy White
Serious	John McEnroe
Crying with Laughter	Bob Monkhouse
The Life and Times of the Thunderbolt Kid	Bill Bryson
Quite Contrary	Mary Whitehouse
My Booky Wook	Russell Brand
All Creatures Great and Small	James Herriot
The Downing Street Years	Margaret Thatcher
My Tune	Simon Bates
Dreams from My Father: A Story of Race and Inheritance	Barack Obama
Laughing and Laughing	Michael McIntyre
Walking on Water	Brian Clough
Managing My Life	Sir Alex Ferguson
Unless I'm very much mistaken	Murray Walker
Robbie Williams: Somebody, Someday	Robbie Williams
A Journey	Tony Blair

Nothing Like a Dame	Thora Hird
Learning to Fly	Victoria Beckham
Trowel and Error	Alan Titchmarsh
The Diary of a Young Girl	Ann Frank

All of these are written by famous people and consequently of huge interest to many. Our own stories may not quite capture the public imagination in the same way, but we all have a story to tell – our own unique experiences, our own journey through life – and as Christians that includes a story of faith: the way God called us to respond to his love in Christ; the way he has led us over the years; the way he has nurtured, strengthened, comforted and inspired, leading us to where we are today. As we stand on the threshold of another year, this is an opportunity to reflect on such things, and, in remembering God's faithfulness, to look forward to another chapter in our own continuing story. We do not know how the plot will unravel in the days ahead, what new pages might be written, but we do know that we can trust the author of life itself and the one who has written our names in the pages of the book of life.

Looking to the Future

Readings   Jeremiah 29:10-14; Revelation 21:1-4

Aim   To emphasise that God holds the future in his hands, and that, whatever that future may hold, we can trust him in all things to work for good, sure of his eternal purpose.

Preparation   No special preparation is needed for this talk.

Talk   Ask the congregation what name we give to novels, films or TV programmes set in the future, either depicting what life on earth might become one day or set in far-flung galaxies of the universe. The answer, of course, is science fiction. Tell the congregation that you have prepared a quiz for them with a science-fiction flavour:

- Which long-running television programme follows the fortunes of a Time Lord? *Dr Who*
- Which film had as its chief villain the Emperor Ming? *Flash*
- Which films featured dinosaurs recreated from ancient DNA? *Jurassic Park* (1 and 2)
- Which old TV space series featured a computer called Orac? *Blake's 7*
- Which hugely popular space film spawned two sequels and several prequels? *Star Wars*
- Which book by George Orwell was about a year in the future that is now long past? *1984*
- Which Stephen Spielberg science-fiction film featured a lovable extra-terrestrial? *ET*
- Which Stephen Spielberg film focuses on meetings with aliens? *Close Encounters of the Third Kind*
- Which book by Aldous Huxley warned of dehumanisation in a scientific age? *Brave New World*

- Which humorous space series by Douglas Adams was first broad-cast on the radio? *A Hitch Hiker's Guide to the Galaxy*
- Which series featured Captain Kirk of the Starship Enterprise? *Star Trek*
- Which classic science-fiction book was about giant plants? *The Day of the Triffids*
- What space film is set at the beginning of this millennium? *2001: A Space Odyssey*
- Which classic book is about interplanetary warfare? *The War of the Worlds*
- Which author created the hugely successful *Discworld* series of books? *Terry Pratchett*
- Which Old Testament prophet looked forward to the world of the future? *Jeremiah*
- Which book of the New Testament focuses on last times and God's kingdom? *Revelation*

Each of the above painted a picture of what the world might be like in the future, but all except two represent mere speculation – all, that is, except for Jeremiah and the book of Revelation. Whereas the other authors wrote about what might happen, Jeremiah and Revelation speak of what would happen. In Jeremiah's case, he spoke first to the people of Israel concerning an end to their time in Israel, but his words generally concerning God's plans apply to us and all those who trust in God's purpose. 'For surely I know the plans I have for you, says the Lord, plans for your welfare and not for harm, to give you a future with hope' (Jeremiah 29:11). This, of course, is not to say that we are guaranteed immunity from life's troubles, that everything will work out just as we want, that we are guaranteed good things, but it is to say that ultimately God holds our future in his hands, and that nothing can separate us from his love and eternal blessing. Whatever the future may bring, we can look forward to his kingdom, an unforgettable picture of which is painted in the book of Revelation. We do not know every detail of the future, either in this life or the life to come, but we know that God will be with us every step of the way, and that his promise will not fail. In that assurance, let us welcome this new year with hope, confidence, trust and thanksgiving.

New Beginnings

Reading   2 Corinthians 5:16-21

Aim   To bring home the fact that with God not just every year but every day and moment is a new beginning.

Preparation   Print the following words in large bold letters, and stick them in prominent positions around the church:

LIGHT

PIN

LEAF

WOMAN/MAN

MOON

TRICKS

BROOM

BLOOD

JERSEY

LOOK

ENGLAND

WORLD

BORN

YEAR

Talk   Ask the congregation if they can think of one word that can be applied to all of the words on display. The word you are looking for is NEW. Now ask people to look around at the walls, and to see if they can find the words that match the clues you are going to give them.

1. We talk of seeing something in a new [what?] – *New light*

2. We sometimes use the expression 'as bright as a new [what?]' – *New pin*

3. When we resolve to change, we speak of 'turning over a new [what?]' – *New leaf*

4. When we've recovered from an illness we might talk of 'feeling like a new [what?] or [what?]'? *New woman* or *new man*

5. A lunar phase – *New moon*

6. We sometimes say that 'you can't teach an old dog new [what]'? *New tricks*

7. A new [what?] sweeps clean – *New broom*

8. We sometimes say this is needed if ideas have grown stale – *New blood*

9. This sounds like an addition to our wardrobe but the answer is in fact an American state – *New Jersey*

10. This sounds like you're viewing something but in fact it is a clothes store – *New Look*

11. This sounds close to home but is in fact in America – *New England*

12. This new [what?] sounds like it may harbour extra-terrestrial life but is in fact the name once given to a continent very much on this planet – *New World*

13. This is the term used for recently arrived offspring – *Newborn*

14. This is often seen as the time for resolutions – *New Year*

All of these in some way are, or at least were, about new beginnings, making a fresh start, and of course there is a very strong sense of that in the last example: New Year. This is a time, as indicated in the clue, when many make resolutions, but even if you don't do that there is always, if only briefly, a sense of starting again as we say goodbye to one year and hello to another. Sadly, it doesn't usually last for long, old habits dying hard and both the world and ourselves proving to be much the same despite the passing of another twelve months. Yet at the heart of our faith is the promise that things can be different, that we really can start again, not just at the beginning of the year but at any time, any moment of our lives. As Paul puts it in his second letter to the Corinthians (5:17): 'If anyone is in Christ, there is a new creation: everything old has passed away; see, everything has become new!' It may not always feel like that, for, though ultimately defeated, the old self lives on, repeatedly rearing its ugly head, but God is always ready to wipe the slate clean and give us another opportunity. That is the conviction in which we enter this new year: that ours is a God able to make us new; a God who, however often we fail, will be ready to pick us up, forgive us, and help us to start again.

Week of Prayer for Christian Unity

Working Together

Reading 1 Corinthians 12:4-6, 12-13

Aim Using the analogy of an orchestra, to bring home the fact that Christians of all denominations have a vital part to play in God's purpose, working in harmony together.

Preparation Print in large letters on pieces of card the following words, one for each instrument:

> FLUTE, HARP, TROMBONE, DRUM, TRIANGLE, HORN, TUBA, HARPSICHORD, CELLO, BASSOON, DOUBLE BASS, VIOLA, CLARINET, OBOE, TRUMPET, PIANO, VIOLIN, CYMBALS

Attach a piece of magnetic tape to the back of each.

Talk Tell the congregation you have prepared a quiz for them. From the clues you are about to give, they have to guess which orchestral instruments you are referring to. As each answer is given, set out the answers exactly as they are displayed on the next page. Take care to align them precisely.

1. A woodwind instrument which you hold sideways – *FLUTE*
2. A stringed instrument which is plucked – *HARP*
3. A brass instrument often used in jazz – *TROMBONE*
4. An instrument which is hit with sticks – *DRUM*
5. Sounds like a geometrical shape – *TRIANGLE*
6. Sounds like part of a car – *HORN*
7. A large and heavy brass instrument – *TUBA*
8. A keyboard instrument that is plucked – *HARPSICHORD*
9. A stringed instrument rhyming with hello – *CELLO*

10. The largest and deepest woodwind instrument – *BASSOON*

11. The largest and deepest stringed instrument – *DOUBLE BASS*

12. Sounds like a flower – *VIOLA*

13. A woodwind instrument often used in jazz – *CLARINET*

14. A woodwind instrument which has a double reed – *OBOE*

15. An instrument which you might find in a brass band – *TRUMPET*

16. A keyboard instrument, the Latin word for which means 'soft' – *PIANO*

17. The instrument played by Nigel Kennedy – *VIOLIN*

18. Flat dishes which clang together – *CYMBALS*

```
        F L U T E
            H A R P
T R O M B O N E
        D R U M
T R I A N G L E
        H O R N

          T U B A
H A R P S I C H O R D
          C E L L O
  B A S S O O N
D O U B L E   B A S S

    V I O L A
    C L A R I N E T
    O B O E

    T R U M P E T
      P I A N O
  V I O L I N
      C Y M B A L S
```

Ask if anyone in the congregation can spot the hidden message – THOUGH THESE ARE MANY. Now, tell the congregation you are going to rearrange the words to finish off the hidden message.

Rearrange as follows, again taking care to align the words precisely:

```
                        T  R  O  M  B  O  N  E
         B  A  S  S  O  O  N
         T  R  I  A  N  G  L  E
               F  L  U  T  E
   C  L  A  R  I  N  E  T
                        H  O  R  N
            O  B  O  E
            D  R  U  M

                        T  U  B  A
   H  A  R  P  S  I  C  H  O  R  D
                  C  E  L  L  O
                  C  Y  M  B  A  L  S

            P  I  A  N  O
            H  A  R  P
   D  O  U  B  L  E     B  A  S  S

            V  I  O  L  A
         V  I  O  L  I  N
   T  R  U  M  P  E  T
```

Ask if anybody can see the second part of the message – TOGETHER THEY ARE ONE.

THOUGH THESE ARE MANY, TOGETHER THEY ARE ONE. And of course that is exactly right, for put these instruments together and they form a single orchestra.

What of the Church? How far do these words apply there? As individual Christians we are certainly many, each of us different, with our own ideas and own experiences of God, but through Christ we have been joined together to form one people, one fellowship.

But it doesn't end there, for there are many other Christians outside our own fellowship, both within our particular denomination and beyond. The fact is that Christians have different ways of doing things, different ways of worshipping, different types of service, and sometimes even different interpretations of various aspects of faith.

But though we are many, we are still nonetheless one, all serving the same God, all part of the same family, all working for the same kingdom. We may have different roles and different contributions to make, but it is only when we work together that God's purpose can finally be complete.

Bound Together

Readings   Ephesians 4:15-16; 1 Corinthians 12:1-13, 27-31

Aim   To recognise our differences as Christians, but also to emphasise the unity that should characterise the Church.

Preparation   For this talk, you will need the following (empty containers/packets will do for many): wallpaper paste, glue stick, sticky tack, bonding adhesive, Copydex, wood glue, UHU glue, sticky tape, parcel tape, superglue, a small quantity of cement.

Talk   Tell the congregation that you have a talk this week that will have them glued to their seats! Display the various items you have collected together and ask what they have in common. The answer, of course, is that they all stick things together – only it's not quite that simple. Ask which of us, for example, would try to stick paper with cement, or to cement bricks with wallpaper paste, or to hang wallpaper with sticky tack? None of us would even consider it. Different jobs require different glues if they're to be done properly; there is a right one for each. Go through each item, and ask what sort of sticking job people might use it for.

There's a simple lesson in all this for the Church, because like these various adhesives we are all different. That's what Paul was saying in his letter to the Corinthians: we are not the same; each of us are designed by God for a particular role, a certain function. Yet we are all nonetheless one. Just as the items we looked at were all adhesives, so we are all Christians.

And that leads to a second point, and the reason why this talk is about glue, sticky tape and so on, for just as these fasten things together so we should be bound together by the love of Christ. As Paul wrote to the Ephesians (4:15-16, own translation):

Lovingly speaking the truth, we must in every aspect grow up into the head; that is, into Christ; through whom each part of the body – joined and knitted together by its supporting ligaments so that each may function as it should – grows and builds itself up in love.

There is no need for different kinds of adhesives here: the glue that binds us together, irrespective of our differences, is the love of Christ. So then, in this week of prayer for Christian Unity, let us respect our diversity yet remember our unity, recognising that whatever may divide us we are all united in the same Lord, the same faith, the same love.

Though We Are Many

Reading   1 Corinthians 12:4-6, 12-13

Aim   To bring home the fact that truth can be expressed in many different ways, a fact reflected in the diversity of the Church.

Preparation   For this talk you will need various translations of the Bible, each open or marked at the appropriate place, or, perhaps better, you can print translations of the verses below. In either case, do not reveal when reading the passages which translation you are reading from.

New Revised Standard Version

Now there are varieties of gifts, but the same Spirit; and there are varieties of services, but the same Lord; and there are varieties of activities, but it is the same God who activates all of them in every-one. For just as the body is one and has many members, and all the members of the body, though many, are one body, so it is with Christ. For in the one Spirit, we were all baptised into one body – Jews or Greeks, slaves or free – and we were all made to drink of one Spirit.

Authorised Version (King James)

Now there are diversities of gifts, but the same Spirit. And there are differences of administrations, but the same Lord. And there are diversities of operations, but it is the same God which worketh all in all. For as the body is one, and hath many members, and all the members of that one body, being many, are one body: so also is Christ. For by one Spirit we are all baptised into one body, whether we be Jews or Gentiles, whether we be bond or free: and have been all made to drink into one Spirit.

New International Version

There are different kinds of gifts, but the same Spirit. There are different kinds of service, but the same Lord. There are different kinds of working, but the same God works all of them in all men. The body is a unit, though it is made up of many parts; and though all its parts are many, they form one body. So it is with Christ. For we were all baptised by one Spirit into one body – whether Jews or Greeks, slave or free – and we were all given the one Spirit to drink.

New English Bible

There are varieties of gifts, but the same Spirit. There are varieties of service, but the same Lord. There are many forms of work, but all of them, in all men, are the work of the same God. For Christ is like a single body with its many limbs and organs, which, many as they are, together make up one body. For indeed we were all brought into one body by baptism, in the one Spirit, whether we are Jews or Greeks, whether slaves or free men, and that one Holy Spirit was poured out for all of us to drink.

Jerusalem Bible

There is a variety of gifts but always the same Spirit; there are all sorts of service to be done, but always to the same Lord; working in all sorts of different ways in different people, it is the same God who is working in all of them. Just as a human body, though it is made up of many parts, is a single unit because all these parts, though many, make one body, so it is with Christ. In the one Spirit we were all baptised, Jews as well as Greeks, slaves as well as citizens, and one Spirit was given to us all to drink.

You also need to print the following on separate strips of paper, and display them on a whiteboard, using sticky tack or magnetic tape so that you can rearrange them as necessary.

New Revised Standard Version (NRSV)

Authorised Version (or AV, or King James Bible)

New International Version (NIV)

New English Bible (NEB)

Jerusalem Bible

(You may wish to add your own versions and corresponding translations of the verse in question, to complement the list above.)

Talk Tell the congregation that you are going to read them some verses from the Bible, and that you want them to identify which translation they are taken from. Display the list of alternatives you prepared earlier, and then, reading the various translations in turn, take a show of hands each time concerning the translation you are using. Rearrange the list of translations, in the order the congregation decides on. Afterwards, run through the readings again, giving the correct translation (and reordering your display) as necessary.

Ask which was the correct version. Of course, none of them is either correct or incorrect, each being a translation, and therefore interpretation, of the original Greek text, which itself is an attempt to interpret a God-given insight through words. The fact is that there are many ways of expressing the same truth, all of which are equally valid.

That's a lesson we need to keep constantly in mind when it comes to thinking about the Church. Despite the efforts that have been made over the years to break down barriers between Christians, the Church is still fragmented into different groups: Anglicans, Catholics, Evangelicals, Liberals, High Church, Low Church, Traditionalists, Charismatics, to name but a few. So which are right and which are wrong? Which have the truth and which are misguided? The answer once again, of course, is all and none of them. Each expresses in different ways the truth of the gospel, bringing different experiences, histories, insights and characteristics to bear on their interpretation. None has the whole truth but all strive after it. Just as there are many translations but one Bible, so there are many denominations but one Church. Together, we give expression to the love of God made known and experienced through Jesus Christ our Lord.

Mothering
Sunday

Loving Hands

Readings Psalm 31:9-24; Isaiah 42:5-9

Aim To bring home the fact that God holds each one of us in his hands, and to explore the implications of what that means. (The talk is well complemented by the hymn 'I trust in thee, O Lord'.)

Preparation For this talk you will need to either copy, and perhaps enlarge, the pictures shown under Talk, below, or prepare similar illustrations of your own. (Larger photocopiable versions of the pictures given here may be found on pages 44-49.) You will also need to write or print the following Bible verses (from a variety of translations) in large bold letters on to the largest sheets of paper you can find, sticking these up in prominent positions around the church.

> As a mother comforts her child, so will I comfort you. (Isaiah 66:13a)

> Our steps are made firm by the Lord, when he delights in our way; though we stumble, we shall not fall headlong, for the Lord holds us by the hand. (Psalm 37:23-24)

> I am always with you; you hold me by my right hand. You guide me with your counsel. (Psalm 73:23-24a)

> I am the Lord your God, who takes hold of your right hand and says to you, 'Do not fear, I will help you.' (Isaiah 41:13)

> Be strong and courageous. Do not be afraid, do not be discouraged, for the Lord your God will be with you wherever you go. (Joshua 1:9)

> See, the Sovereign Lord comes with power . . . He tends his flock like a shepherd; he gathers the lambs in his arms and carries them close to his heart. (Isaiah 40:10a, 11)

My child, do not despise the Lord's discipline, and do not resent his rebuke, because the Lord disciplines those he loves. (Proverbs 3:11-12)

Every good and perfect gift is from above, coming down from the Father. (James 1:17)

He makes grass grow for the cattle, and plants for man to cultivate – bringing forth food from the earth, bread that sustains the heart. All look to you to give them their food at the proper time. When you give it to them, they gather it up; when you open your hand, they are satisfied with good things. (Psalm 104:14-15, 28)

Why worry about clothes? Look how the wild flowers grow: they do not work or make clothes for themselves. But I tell you that not even Solomon with all his wealth had clothes as beautiful as these flowers. It is God who clothes the wild grass . . . Won't he be all the more sure to clothe you? (Matthew 6:28-30)

Now then, my children, listen to me. Listen to my instruction and be wise, do not ignore it. (Proverbs 8:32)

I will look after those that are lost, bring back those that wander off, bandage those who are hurt, and heal those that are sick. (Ezekiel 34:16)

Talk   Tell the congregation that you want to think today about hands, and what these say to us about mothers and about God. Ask first whether anyone can identify commonly used expressions, all containing the word 'hand' from the following clues:

- Under control – *In hand*
- Being there when needed – *On hand*
- Applies discipline when necessary – *A firm hand*
- Involved in the action, not at a distance – *Hands on*
- Something given free – *Handout*
- Specially and personally chosen – *Hand-picked*
- Given carte blanche; complete discretion – *A free hand*

- Assured of safe keeping, being well looked after – *In good hands*
- Associated with Christian healing – *The laying on of hands*
- Sharing the load, offering help – *Lending a hand*
- A sign of welcome – *Handshake*
- Identifying with a person or people – *Throwing in one's hand with someone*
- Describes something we have made – *Handiwork* (or *handicraft*)

These are all expressions that we can apply in different ways to mothers. To illustrate this look at the following pictures of a mother and child, and see if you can guess what the mother is doing in each case.

Comforting

Supporting

Guiding

Keeping safe/protecting

 *Reassuring*

 *Embracing/holding*

Disciplining/telling off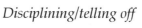

 *Giving*

Providing

 *Clothing*

 *Teaching*

 *Tending*

These are just some of the many ways in which mothers care for and look after us, sometimes not only during childhood but beyond. But if they apply to mothers, they apply also to God, as the various verses displayed around the church show. (Run through the pictures again, asking if anyone can find a verse to match each one.)

Comforting

As a mother comforts her child, so will I comfort you. (Isaiah 66:13a)

Supporting

Our steps are made firm by the Lord, when he delights in our way; though we stumble, we shall not fall headlong, for the Lord holds us by the hand. (Psalm 37:23-24)

Guiding

I am always with you; you hold me by my right hand. You guide me with your counsel. (Psalm 73:23-24a)

Keeping safe/protecting

I am the Lord your God, who takes hold of your right hand and says to you, 'Do not fear, I will help you.' (Isaiah 41:13)

Reassuring

Be strong and courageous. Do not be afraid, do not be discouraged, for the Lord your God will be with you wherever you go. (Joshua 1:9)

Embracing/holding

See, the Sovereign Lord comes with power . . . He tends his flock like a shepherd; he gathers the lambs in his arms and carries them close to his heart. (Isaiah 40:10a, 11)

Disciplining/telling off

My child, do not despise the Lord's discipline, and do not resent his rebuke, because the Lord disciplines those he loves. (Proverbs 3:11-12)

Giving

Every good and perfect gift is from above, coming down from the Father. (James 1:17)

Providing

He makes grass grow for the cattle, and plants for man to cultivate – bringing forth food from the earth, bread that sustains the heart. All look to you to give them their food at the proper time. When you give it to them, they gather it up; when you open your hand, they are satisfied with good things. (Psalm 104:14-15, 28)

Clothing

Why worry about clothes? Look how the wild flowers grow: they do not work or make clothes for themselves. But I tell you that not even Solomon with all his wealth had clothes as beautiful as these flowers. It is God who clothes the wild grass . . . Won't he be all the more sure to clothe you? (Matthew 6:28-30)

Teaching

Now then, my children, listen to me. Listen to my instruction and be wise, do not ignore it. (Proverbs 8:32)

Tending

I will look after those that are lost, bring back those that wander off, bandage those who are hurt, and heal those that are sick. (Ezekiel 34:16)

In other words, mothers aren't alone in caring for us in these ways; God does too. Today is a day for remembering mothers – for sending cards, giving flowers or simply expressing how much they mean or meant to us – but it is also a day for remembering how much God loves us and values us as his children. So we can gladly join with David in saying, 'I trust in you, O Lord; I acknowledge that you are my God; my times are in your hands' (Psalm 31:14, own translation).

Learning from Mothers

Readings   Various Bible verses are integral to this talk (see under Preparation and Talk).

Aim   To consider what a mother's love can teach us about the love God has for us.

Preparation   On large sheets of paper, print the following in bold, clearly visible letters and display in different positions around the church. Allow sufficient space for the missing word to be inserted later in the talk.

As a mother comforts her child, so I will _____ you. (Isaiah 66:13)

The Lord is good, his steadfast _____ endures for ever. (Psalm 100:5)

My child, do not despise the Lord's _____. (Proverbs 3:11)

God is our refuge and strength, a very present _____ in trouble. (Psalm 46:1)

God himself will _____ the lamb. (Genesis 22:8a)

_____ the weak hands, and make firm the feeble knees. (Isaiah 35:3)

I will _____ over them to build and to plant, says the Lord. (Jeremiah 31:28b)

Come, let us return to the Lord . . . and he will _____ us. (Hosea 6:1)

_____ me, O God, for in you I take refuge. (Psalm 16:1)

Cast all your anxiety on him, because he _____ for you. (1 Peter 5:7)

He will come and _____ you. (Isaiah 35:4b)

The Lord will _____ you continually. (Isaiah 58:11a)

If we confess our sins, he who is faithful and just will _____us. (1 John 1:9a)

He will _____ his flock like a shepherd. (Isaiah 40:11a)

I will instruct you and _____ you the way you should go. (Psalm 32:8a)

Give ear, O Lord, to my prayer; _____ to my cry of supplication. (Psalm 86:6)

If God so clothes the grass of the field . . . how much more will he_____ you. (Luke 12:28)

On separate pieces of card, print the letters comprising the wordsearch on the following page, using the same-size lettering as in the Bible verses above, and arrange on a whiteboard as shown, using sticky tack to stick the letters to the board.

N	E	H	T	G	N	E	R	T	S
P	L	O	V	E	H	C	T	A	W
R	E	L	I	S	T	E	N	F	E
O	H	F	S	E	R	A	C	O	D
T	T	E	H	E	L	P	H	R	I
E	O	E	E	V	A	S	H	G	V
C	L	D	H	E	A	L	A	I	O
T	C	G	U	I	D	E	E	V	R
T	R	O	F	M	O	C	T	E	P
D	I	S	C	I	P	L	I	N	E

Talk Ask what are the first two words of the Lord's Prayer. The answer, of course, is 'Our Father', and that is the way we tend to think of God: as a father. Announce that, because today is Mothering Sunday, you want instead to consider God in terms of motherhood, asking what we might learn from mothers about who and what God is like. Explain that you have prepared a word-search to help you do that. It contains 17 words that describe the sort of things mothers do or feel for us. Ask if people can find them and then find a verse somewhere in the church in which the word they have found fits. When they have done so, remove the appropriate letters from the board and reassemble them to fill in the missing word in the Bible verse. The complete verses are as follows:

As a mother comforts her child, so I will COMFORT you. (Isaiah 66:13)

The Lord is good; his steadfast LOVE endures for ever. (Psalm 100:5)

My child, do not despise the Lord's DISCIPLINE. (Proverbs 3:11)

God is our refuge and strength, a very present HELP in trouble. (Psalm 46:1)

God himself will PROVIDE the lamb. (Genesis 22:8a)

STRENGTHEN the weak hands, and make firm the feeble knees. (Isaiah 35:3)

I will WATCH over them to build and to plant, says the Lord. (Jeremiah 31:28b)

Come, let us return to the Lord . . . and he will HEAL us. (Hosea 6:1a)

PROTECT me, O God, for in you I take refuge. (Psalm 16:1)

Cast all your anxiety on him, because he CARES for you. (1 Peter 5:7)

He will come and SAVE you. (Isaiah 35:4b)

The Lord will GUIDE you continually. (Isaiah 58:11a)

If we confess our sins, he who is faithful and just will FORGIVE us. (1 John 1:9a)

He will FEED his flock like a shepherd. (Isaiah 40:11a)

I will instruct you and TEACH you the way you should go. (Psalm 32:8a)

Give ear, O Lord, to my prayer; LISTEN to my cry of supplication. (Psalm 86:6)

If God so clothes the grass of the field . . . how much more will he CLOTHE you. (Luke 12:28)

We celebrate Mothering Sunday for two reasons. First, it reminds us of how much mothers do for us – the sort of things we have thought of today. Second, the example set by mothers reminds us how God loves and cares for us in turn, watching over us and caring for us in a multitude of ways. Give thanks for mothers, give thanks to God, and celebrate all that they mean and do within our lives.

Christian Aid Week

Neighbours

Reading Luke 10:25-37

Aim To bring home the fact that, in God's eyes, anyone in need is potentially our neighbour.

Preparation No special preparation is needed for this talk.

Talk Ask where would you find the following living as neighbours? (Given that soap-opera characters are constantly changing, you may need to substitute different names to those given in the lists below.)

- *Ramsay Street*
  Harold Bishop
  Susan Kennedy
  Brad Willis
  Amber Turner

- *Albert Square*
  Bianca Jackson
  Phil Mitchell
  Ian Beale
  Kat Slater

- *Coronation Street*
  Amy Barlow
  Kylie Platt
  Eva Price
  Audrey Roberts

- *Emmerdale*
  Edna Birch
  Marlon Dingle
  Carl King
  Katie Sugden

- *Downing Street*
  Prime Minister
  Chancellor of the Exchequer

- *Give the name of the road/street in which your church is situated*
  Give the names of four people living in the same road/street as your church

All of these – even though most are fictitious – are neighbours in the traditional sense of living next door to/or in the same street/vicinity as each other. But the word 'neighbour' or 'neighbouring' can be understood in a much broader sense. Can anyone, for example, think of the county, country and continent respectively that is neighbour to the following:

- *Gloucestershire, Wiltshire, Berkshire, Buckinghamshire, Northamptonshire and Warwickshire*
  Oxfordshire

- *France, Germany, The Netherlands*
  Belgium

- *North America*
  South America

Neighbours are not necessarily those living next door. It's a commonplace to observe that we live in a small world, but today, in our internet and satellite age, that's more true than ever. So who is our neighbour in a context such as this? According to Jesus, the answer is simple: it is anyone we come across in need. Whether it is somebody down our street or living in some distant continent, through responding to their need we honour the commandment to love our neighbour as ourselves.

That, essentially, is what Christian Aid reminds us of. It highlights the plight of the poor in so many parts of our world: people we will never meet, countries we will probably never visit, and situations we may quite possibly never fully understand, yet those within them are our neighbours in need of our help. We cannot respond to all, but we cannot and should not ignore them either. As Jesus himself reminds us, when we respond to even one person, we respond also to him. We are challenged today to recognise our common humanity, and to respond as neighbours.

A Raw Deal

Reading   Matthew 25:1-46

Aim   To illustrate the inequalities of this world and the unfairness underlying them, and to ask in what way we intend to respond to these.

Preparation   You will need two packs of playing cards. Prepare one pack so that when you deal two hands of thirteen cards each, starting from the top, the first hand ends up with four 2's, four 3's, four 4's, and a 5, while the second hands ends up with four Aces, four Kings, four Queens, and one Jack in the same suit as the five in hand one. From the second pack, prepare two more hands (for display purposes only), the first having three Aces, three Kings, three Queens, and a Jack (use hearts, diamonds and clubs only) and the second having a complete set of spades, two up to Ace.

Talk   Tell the congregation you fancy playing a game of cards and ask if anyone is willing to play a hand with you? Select a volunteer (making sure they are old enough to understand the basic rules of whist) and then deal out two hands from the first pack you rigged earlier. Give the first hand to the volunteer and keep the second for yourself. Explain that you will be playing by the rules of whist (i.e. Aces high, trumping allowed only when unable to follow suit). Announce to the congregation that you are going to choose trumps (the suit that you have four cards of) and then tell them that, to make things more interesting for them, you are going to show them the two hands first! Display both hands of cards and ask whether the congregation thinks the game will be a fair contest. Light-heartedly brush off their protests, and proceed to play. You will, of course, win every trick!

Express sympathy with your opponent and thank them for their help. Display the other two sets of hands that you prepared before the service, and ask the congregation if this would give a fairer game. The answer this time depends on who chooses trumps. If your opponent chooses, he or she will win every trick; if you choose, then you will win them all.

What has all this to do with Christian Aid, you may ask – and if you put this question to the congregation, you may very well get some intelligent answers offering a useful lead-in to the rest of the talk! The answer is that, in terms of the world as a whole, we are those who have been dealt a good hand; those who hold all the cards when it comes to securing the spoils. We may not be rich compared to many in this country, but compared to the majority in what we call the Third World, we are those who have been dealt all the cards, who are incomparably wealthy. Do we recognise how fortunate we are? Do we remember those less fortunate? Do we give from our plenty so that all may have some share in this earth's bounty?

There's a second and more disturbing point to be made, arising from the second set of hands we looked at, for what we saw there was that who wins depends on who has first choice; on who, in other words, holds the power in the contest. In terms of world affairs and economic systems, the answer to that is very clear: for centuries it has been the Western world that has called the tune, and those whom we label the Third World have been engaged in a game of catch-up that they haven't the slightest hope of winning. Power rests firmly in the hands of prosperous nations and their governments, and, more recently, in the hands of giant corporations and multi-nationals; the pack is loaded against so-called developing countries. We all know, if we are honest, that we are part of an unjust world, a divided world of rich and poor, well-fed and hungry, haves and have-nots. What are we going to do about it? What response are we, personally, going to make?

Actions Speak Louder Than Words

Readings	Matthew 25:31-46; James 1:22-27; 2:14-17
Aim	To emphasise the importance of showing our faith in action.
Preparation	No special preparation is needed for this talk, but you may want to practise making the gestures indicated under 'Talk', perhaps using a mirror or asking a friend if he or she can recognise what you are trying to say.
Talk	Tell the congregation that instead of talking to them you are going to try instead to communicate without using words. Ask if anyone can tell what the following gestures mean:

Put finger to your lips	*Shush, be quiet*
Make beckoning gesture	*Come here*
Wave the back of your hands	*Go away*
Put hands up, palms forward	*Stop*
Shake fist	*I'll get you*
Cover both eyes with your hands	*How embarrassing*
Wagging finger	*Telling someone off*
Thumbs up	*Everything's OK*
Thumbs down	*It's no good/hasn't worked*
Scratch your head	*I'm thinking*
Yawn	*I'm tired*
Clap hands	*Applause*
Bow	*Taking the plaudits*
Hold up hands, palms a fraction apart	*It's this small*
Hold arms wide apart, palms turned in	*It's this big*

Put one finger in each ear	*Keep the noise down, you're deafening me*
Cup a hand behind your ear	*I can't hear you*
Place hand horizontally above eyes	*I can't quite see it; it's there somewhere*
Point a finger	*It's over there*
Shrug your shoulders	*I don't know, no idea*
Pretend to shake hands	*Hello, pleased to meet you*
Make circular motion with hand	*I'm slowing down* (when driving)
Punch the air with clenched fist/s	*I've won!*
Shake arm about in front of you	*Four runs* (cricket umpire's signal)
Raise outstretched hands to sky	*Six runs* (cricket umpire's signal)
Make an army salute	*Sir*

All of these illustrate that we can communicate powerfully without using words. In fact, a smile, wink, frown or glare can often say more than words can even begin to; hence the often-used expression 'actions speak louder than words'. Paradoxically, words can actually get in the way of communication, saying one thing while our actions say another. We might speak kindly while looking daggers at someone, preach kindness yet be the meanest person imaginable, talk of integrity but be dishonest in our dealings with others. All of which perhaps explains why the Bible has so much to say on the subject of our deeds marrying up with our words. 'Dear children,' we read in 1 John 3:18, 'let us not love with words or tongue but with actions and in truth.' Or, as James puts it (1:22; 2:17), 'Do not merely listen to the word, and so deceive yourselves. Do what it says . . . Faith by itself, if it is not accompanied by action, is dead.'

In other words, being a Christian means more than simply saying the right words. Yes, confession of faith is part of it, and no, God doesn't expect us to be perfect, but if we're serious about following Jesus, then something of him should show in our lives. According to Matthew, that 'something' should be a concern for others that makes itself visible through practical acts of caring, whether responding to the hungry, ensuring a supply of water for the thirsty, visiting the sick, providing clothes for those in need or responding to the persecuted. Through deeds such as these, faith shows itself in action. We may not have such needs on our doorstep, but there are numerous examples in the wider world – examples brought to our attention by such agencies as Christian Aid. In a world where the gulf between rich and poor grows ever wider, where millions go hungry and thirsty, and where nations still struggle with the burden of poverty and disease, the call to respond is as urgent as ever.

It's easy to talk about such things, to express dismay, to speak about the need for reform, and so on, but eventually it needs actions as well as words to change things, and it is actions rather than words that will testify to the reality of our faith. Do we respond meaningfully, generously, sacrificially to those in whose suffering Christ is crying out to us? Do we show through our actions that our concern for them is real? Actions speak louder than words; so what do your actions say to others about your faith?

Father's Day

Responding to the Father

Reading Luke 15:11-32

Aim To highlight the fatherly love of God, and to respond in praise and worship.

Preparation On separate strips of card / paper, print the following lines of hymns. Ensure that the keywords highlighted in bold are roughly the same width by using larger letters where the word is short and small letters where it is long. If possible, highlight the keywords in a different colour. Avoid turnover lines if possible, but if any are needed ensure they do not overlap the keyword.

Dear Lord and Father of mankind

Father **God** I wonder how I managed to exist

We come unto **our** fathers' God

Great is thy faithfulness, O God my Father

Father whose mighty word, chaos **and** darkness heard

Lead us, **heavenly** Father, lead us

Eternal **Father**, strong to save

Father, hear the prayer **we** offer

Our Father God, thy name we **praise**

Abba Father, let me be yours, **and** yours alone

Father, we love you, we **worship** and adore you

Father, we adore **you**

For the might of your arm we bless you, our God, our fathers' God

Father, I place into **your** hands the things that I can't do

Of the Father's **love** begotten

Using pieces of sticky tack, stick up the hymn lines in prominent positions around the church. You will also need to enlist the help of your church organist or pianist for this talk. Give them a copy of the list of hymns, and prime them to play the first two lines of each as part of a *Name that tune quiz* during the talk.

Talk Tell the congregation that you have something different for them today – a Father's Day version of the old musical quiz-show *Name that tune*. Explain that the organist/pianist is going to play the first lines of some well-known hymns and worship songs, all of which have the word 'Father' or 'fathers' in them. Their job is to identify the first line or lines of the hymn from the tune. As an extra clue, the various lines are displayed around the walls of the church.

Ask the organist/pianist, to play the first tune. If this is named correctly, ask if anyone can spot the line somewhere in the church. Invite whoever puts his or her hand up first to take it off the wall and bring it to you. Stick this on to a whiteboard, positioning it carefully as shown on pages 73-74. Continue in the same way for each of the various hymns, ensuring that the keyword in each hymn title lines up below the one above.

When each tune has been identified, thank the organist/pianist and all those who have helped you, and then read through the list of hymns again. Each one celebrates God as our Father or speaks of him as our fathers' God, and both of those ideas are appropriate themes for Father's Day. On the one hand, we are here to think of fathers, to remember all we owe to them and to express our appreciation of all they mean or once meant to us. This is a day that calls fathers to consider their responsibilities, and children to consider their response.

It is impossible, though, to think of fathers without also thinking of 'Our Father': as Jesus encouraged us to picture God. Throughout the Scriptures we find him described in this way, and perhaps nowhere is what that means better illustrated than in the parable Jesus told of the lost or prodigal son. We call it that, but, as many have observed, the parable is as much about the father as the son; the father who, it seems, looks out longingly each day in the hope of seeing his child returning, and who, when he does this, runs out with open arms to greet him and welcome him home. That's the God we serve: not stern, remote and forbidding, but full of love, yearning to draw us close, always ready to forgive and forget, constantly looking to restore our relationship with him however often we might break it. Ours is a God who guides, loves, saves and protects, faithfully watching over us, his nature always to have mercy. That's why so many of the hymns and songs we sing today acknowledge him as Father, and that's what these hymns we've identified today are all about. But, as you've probably already spotted, this particular selection has one more thing to say to us as well. (Ask someone to read the highlighted words, from top to bottom.) 'Dear God our great and heavenly Father, we praise and worship you for your love.' A simple prayer through which we can respond and express our gratitude for everything that God has done for us. (Finish the talk by inviting the congregation to join with you in saying the prayer together. See pages 72-73.)

MORE ALL-AGE TALKS FOR *Special* SUNDAYS

Dear Lord and Father of mankind

Father **God** I wonder how I managed to exist

We come unto **our** fathers' God

Great is thy faithfulness, O God my Father

Father whose mighty word, chaos **and darkness heard**

Lead us, **heavenly** Father, lead us

Eternal **Father**, strong to save

Father, hear the prayer **we** offer

Our Father God, thy name we **praise**

Abba Father, let me be yours, **and** yours alone

Father, we love you, we **worship** and adore you

Father, we adore you

For the might of your arm we bless you, our God, our fathers' God

Father, I place into **your** hands the things that I can't do

Of the Father's **love** begotten

The Father of All

Readings   Ephesians 4:1-6; Romans 8:12-17

Aim   To celebrate the part fathers play in our lives and to recognise that God is the Father of all.

Preparation   Print on individual pieces of card/paper the letters in the word-search below and arrange them carefully on a whiteboard as shown. Fix them with a single small piece of sticky tack so that they can be removed easily during the talk.

N	W	O	R	B	T	T	R	S	H	E	G
R	C	N	A	M	I	E	E	R	Y	I	R
M	H	E	S	O	M	N	H	E	M	E	A
A	R	G	S	O	E	R	T	H	R	M	N
I	I	S	D	U	A	A	A	T	A	A	D
L	S	N	A	G	O	D	F	A	F	H	F
L	T	G	U	U	A	H	D	F	D	A	A
I	M	S	I	T	C	H	O	E	A	R	T
W	A	E	R	B	O	E	G	R	Y	B	H
F	S	S	E	M	A	H	T	O	A	A	E
L	O	N	G	L	E	G	S	F	L	L	R

Talk   Tell the congregation that you have a simple combined quiz and word-search for them. All the questions/clues are concerned with dads or fathers, and the answers (given here in italics) point to the words hidden in the word-search. (The words to look for in the latter are highlighted in capitals.) As each answer is given and subsequently found in the word-search, remove the appropriate letters of the word from the board and discard them. The clues are as follows:

- A personification of the passing of the years: *Old Father TIME*

- 'You are old, Father _____', the young man said: *WILLIAM*

- Another name for the second-longest river in Britain: *Old Father THAMES*

- A venerable Smurf: *Father ABRAHAM*

- A priest-cum-detective created by G. K. Chesterton: *Father BROWN*

- This well-loved character is associated with a special season: *Father CHRISTMAS*

- The name given to the longest serving member in the House of Commons: *Father of the HOUSE*

- According to Wordsworth, 'the child is _____': *father of the MAN*

- Another name for our ancestors: *FOREFATHERS*

- A large old-fashioned timepiece: *GRANDFATHER clock*

- Either a male sponsor at a child's baptism or the head of a mafia gang: *GODFATHER*

- The name given to the Home Guard during the Second World War: *Dad's ARMY*

- Another name for the crane fly and the harvestman: *Daddy-LONGLEGS*

- A one-time larger-than-life wrestler: *BIG Daddy*

- The name given to a middle-aged or elderly man who showers gifts on a much younger woman: *SUGAR Daddy*

- A popular and flavoursome accompaniment to food: Dad's SAUCE

- The occasion we're here to celebrate: *Father's DAY*

At the end of the talk, all that should be left on the board is this:

						T		H	E	
R						E			I	
		S	O			N			E	
	G		O							
		D				A				
	N					D		F		
				A						
			T		H					
	E	R		O						
F								A		
								L	L	

Ask if anyone in the congregation can read what the remaining letters spell, reading from left to right, top to bottom. After someone has identified the text, close up the letters to spell it out more clearly: 'There is one God and Father of all' (Ephesians 4:4a, 6a).

We are here today, of course, to give thanks for fathers – for all they mean or have meant to us – but we are here also to remember the One who is the Father of all, and to give thanks for the love, goodness, grace and mercy he shows to us each day. Don't forget what fathers do. Make a point of showing your appreciation, whenever and wherever you can. Equally, don't forget what God does, what God means, what God has given – and, in turn, show him, through words and deeds, how grateful you are.

Harvest

Gifts of the World

Reading   Psalm 104:1-30

Aim   To bring home the global dimension of Harvest, and to stress the importance of all enjoying a share in what God has given.

Preparation   Print the following in large bold letters on separate slips of paper / card:

> HAWAII, SRI LANKA, ITALY, TURKEY, CHINA, BRAZIL, SAUDI ARABIA, NEW ZEALAND, FRANCE, SOUTH AFRICA, SPAIN, WEST INDIES, SCOTLAND, ORANGES, FIGS, HAGGIS, PINEAPPLES, KIWI FRUIT, OIL, WINE, TEA, COFFEE, PASTA, RICE, DIAMONDS, BANANAS

Attach a small piece of magnetic tape or sticky tack to the back of each slip and arrange them at random on a whiteboard.

Talk   Ask if people can identify matching pairs from the words on the display board. The pairs are as follows:

HAWAII	PINEAPPLES
SRI LANKA	TEA
ITALY	PASTA
TURKEY	FIGS
CHINA	RICE
BRAZIL	COFFEE
SAUDI ARABIA	OIL
NEW ZEALAND	KIWI FRUIT
FRANCE	WINE
SOUTH AFRICA	DIAMONDS
SPAIN	ORANGES
WEST INDIES	BANANAS
SCOTLAND	HAGGIS

Of course, many of these items are grown in places other than the one shown, and many of these countries grow different crops, but this short list provides an important reminder that when we think of and celebrate Harvest today we are talking not just about a local harvest but also about the wider world. Look at the label next time you eat something, and see where it was grown or produced. Apples from South Africa, tea from Sri Lanka, butter from New Zealand – the food we eat derives from various continents, and our modern-day harvest has a global dimension that we cannot and must not ignore. We are part of a wider world in which countries, people and economies are interdependent.

Harvest, then, is a time for celebrating God's creation and giving thanks for the food and plenty we enjoy, but it is a time also for remembering the contribution and needs of others and for resolving to work, so far as we are able, towards a world in which all have a fair share in God's abundant harvest.

A Hidden Harvest Message

Reading   Psalm 65:1, 9-13

Aim   To bring home the fact that Harvest involves human effort that should be appreciated but that it is finally dependent on God.

Preparation   On separate pieces of card or paper, print the following in large bold letters:

TURNIP, HERBS, APPLE, NUTS, KIWI
FRUIT, GRAPES, ONION, DAMSON,
FLOWERS, ORANGE, RHUBARB,
AUBERGINE, LEMON, LEEK

Attach a piece of sticky tack or magnetic tape to the back of each, and retain for use during the talk.

Ensure you have them in order, so that you are not rummaging around to find the correct word during the talk. If possible, arrange for one of each of these to be on display as part of the Harvest produce, ready for you to use as a visual aid. If this is not possible, make a simple line drawing of each fruit and vegetable etc. instead. You will also need some tins and packets of brand-labelled products that can be readily identified by members of the congregation – for example, Walkers crisps, Jacob's cream crackers, Heinz baked beans, HP spaghetti, Princes pineapple pieces, McDougalls flour, Mr Kipling's cakes, John West tuna, KP peanuts, Robertson's jam, Fray Bentos corned beef.

Talk   Hold up each of the brand-labelled products and ask what it is and who made it. The congregation should have little difficulty in identifying each item and its 'manufacturer'. You could be forgiven for thinking, reading the labels, that these products are all man-made, and in a sense they are, because the ingredients within them have been grown or reared by farmers or trawled by fishermen and then processed, canned or so forth by various manufacturers and packagers.

All sorts of people are involved in providing the food we put on our tables, and a proper celebration of Harvest needs to involve a recognition of and thanksgiving for all the work that goes into its production.

But of course, although these products have needed some input, none of them is truly man-made. To illustrate what I mean, identify the following (hold up the fruits and vegetables etc. listed overleaf) and as each is identified, place the matching word on a whiteboard in a column, as shown).

TURNIP
HERBS
APPLE
NUTS
KIWI FRUIT

GRAPES
ONION
DAMSON

FLOWERS
ORANGE
RHUBARB

AUBERGINE
LEMON
LEEK

Ask if anybody can see the message that these fruits, nuts and vegetables convey. The answer, of course, is spelt out by reading the first letter of every word downwards: THANK GOD FOR ALL! This is what Harvest is ultimately all about; it reminds us that although human hands play a very real part in producing the things we eat, God is ultimately the provider and maker of all. Give thanks, then, today for all behind our Harvest, but above all, give thanks to him who makes it all possible.

Looking into Harvest

Readings   Psalm 145 (various Bible verses are also included as part of this talk)

Aim   To explore the various aspects of what Harvest has to say to us today.

Preparation   On separate squares of card, one per letter, print in large bold print the word HARVEST, seven times. Fasten magnetic tape or sticky tack to the back of each letter, and then arrange on a whiteboard to spell the word HARVEST seven times in a column down the left side.

Next, print the following Bible verses (own translation) on large strips of paper, and display in prominent positions around the church:

- The earth has produced its harvest. God, our God, has blessed us! (Psalm 67:6)

- You will have more than enough to eat, and be ... well satisfied. (Joel 2:26)

- My father's hired hands have food in plenty but here am I about to starve. (Luke 15:17).

- They called for help, but nobody was there to save them. (Psalm 18:41)

- God is able to supply you with good things in profusion, so that, invariably having sufficient of everything, you may share lavishly in good works of every kind. (2 Corinthians 9:8)

Talk   Point to the board and tell the congregation that there are no prizes for guessing what you want to talk about: HARVEST! Ask if anyone can think of words we might make out of the letters spelling 'Harvest'. There are numerous possibilities – for example, HEART, VEST, EARS, TEAR, TEA, THE, HAS and STAR. Continue taking suggestions until the ideas start to run short, then tell the congregation that you want to focus on six words (which may have been mentioned or not). The words can be found in the six verses positioned around the church. Read the first verse: 'The earth has produced its harvest. God, our God, has blessed us!' (Psalm 67:6), and ask if anyone can spot the word in question: EARTH. (As each word is correctly identified in the verses, remove the letters from the next complete 'HARVEST' on the board, and rearrange the letters to spell the new word.)

'Earth' could hardly be a more fitting word in relation to Harvest for both its meanings are central to thanksgiving. 'Earth' can mean the soil in which we grow things, providing the vital moisture, minerals and nutrients on which all growth depends. It can also mean the planet on which we live, with all its beauty and variety, wonder and mystery. It is here that Harvest begins: in celebrating the world God has given to us, the life it sustains and the fruitfulness it exhibits.

What about the second of our verses: 'You will have more than enough to eat, and be well satisfied' (Joel 2:26)? The word this time is EAT: and once more this takes us to what Harvest is traditionally all about: a celebration of what God has given us to eat, of the food we enjoy. The fruit, vegetables and other foodstuffs with which we decorate our churches at Harvest represent just a small selection of the good things we eat by God's grace.

But let's go on a bit further, to our third verse: 'My father's hired hands have food in plenty but here am I about to starve' (Luke15:17). There are two words here that we might make from Harvest: one is HAVE and the other is STARVE. The word 'have' reminds us of what Harvest can too easily become: a celebration of our good fortune whilst forgetting the needs of others. We are those who have; even the poorest of us are rich and affluent compared with the hungry of so many in our world. Even while we give thanks now for another rich harvest, thousands today will be starving, millions denied a just reward for their labours or facing another failed harvest and famine.

All of which leads us on to our next verse: 'They called for help, but nobody was there to save them' (Psalm 18:41). The word this time is SAVE, which again can be taken in two ways. We all like to save money, and many of us will probably look in the shops for the best bargains, but sometimes when it comes to buying food or things such as tea and coffee we have to balance saving money with perhaps paying that little extra for fair-trade goods; goods for which those who grew or produced them receive fair payment. Through doing that we can do something, if only a little, to help save some from the horrors of poverty, hunger, oppression and exploitation.

This leads us finally to the last verse: 'God is able to supply you with good things in profusion, so that, invariably having sufficient of everything, you may share lavishly in good works of every kind' (2 Corinthians 9:8). The word here is SHARE, and again it is central to a proper celebration of Harvest, for this should not just be a time for ourselves, enjoying all God has given us, but a time when, recognising how fortunate we are and how much we've been given, we share with others, giving from our plenty to help those who have less.

EARTH, EAT, HAVE, STARVE, SAVE, SHARE: all are part of the true meaning of Harvest and we need to consider the meaning and challenge of each one if we are truly to understand and celebrate what Harvest is all about.

One World Week

All God's People

Readings   Romans 10:5-13; Galatians 3:23-29

Aim   To emphasise that in God's eyes we are all individuals of equal worth, no matter what our colour, culture or creed.

Preparation   Copy and enlarge the following map of the world, or, if preferred, use a copy of your own (a large colour map will make more of a visual impression). Stick this at the front of the church on a wall or display board in a position that is clearly visible to all. (If using your own map, you will need to add the numbers 1-20 as shown.)

Arctic Ocean

15   12   19
EUROPE   9 10
14   11
NORTH   Atlantic   13   ASIA   2   1   Pacific
AMERICA 20   Ocean   5   Ocean
4
3
Pacific Ocean   AFRICA
8 SOUTH   18
AMERICA
6   Indian
17   Ocean   AUSTRALIA 16
& OCEANIA
7

The World

In large bold letters, print the following on separate strips of paper/card:

TOKYO, BEIJING, BANGKOK, CALCUTTA, KATHMANDU, RIO DE JANEIRO, BUENOS AIRES, LIMA, CALAIS, BERLIN, BARCELONA, OSLO, BAGHDAD, VANCOUVER, REYKJAVIK, SYDNEY, PRETORIA, KINSHASA, MOSCOW,

NEW YORK, IRAQI, GERMAN, CHINESE,
BRAZILIAN, FRENCH, NORWEGIAN, THAI,
JAPANESE, AUSTRALIAN, ARGENTINIAN,
INDIAN, PERUVIAN, SPANISH, NEPALESE,
CANADIAN, AMERICAN, ZAIRIAN,
SOUTH AFRICAN, RUSSIAN, ICELANDIC.

Display in prominent positions around the church.

Talk Tell the congregation that since it's One World Week you have prepared a quiz for them about countries and people of the world. All they have to do is identify the country in which each place you name is found, and the nationality of someone from there. After each correct answer (given in italics after the place), ask if anyone can spot the place name and the corresponding nationality displayed somewhere in the church. Ask whoever finds these to bring them to you, and stick each place name in the appropriate position on the board (see the number in parentheses following each country) displaying the nationality below this.

a. KINSHASA (18): ZAIRE, *ZAIRIAN*

b. BARCELONA (11): SPAIN, *SPANISH*

c. LIMA (8): PERU, *PERUVIAN*

d. CALCUTTA (4): INDIA, *INDIAN*

e. REYKJAVIK (15): ICELAND, *ICELANDIC*

f. TOKYO (1): JAPAN, *JAPANESE*

g. OSLO (12): NORWAY, *NORWEGIAN*

h. PRETORIA (17): SOUTH AFRICA: *SOUTH AFRICAN*

i. BEIJING (2): CHINA, *CHINESE*

j. KATHMANDU (5): NEPAL, *NEPALESE*

k. SYDNEY (16): AUSTRALIA, *AUSTRALIAN*

l. BERLIN (10): GERMANY, *GERMAN*

m. MOSCOW (19): RUSSIA, *RUSSIAN*

n. BUENOS AIRES (7): ARGENTINA, *ARGENTINIAN*

o. NEW YORK (20): USA, *AMERICAN*

p. RIO DE JANEIRO (6): BRAZIL, *BRAZILIAN*

q. CALAIS (9): FRANCE, *FRENCH*

r. BAGHDAD (13): IRAQ, *IRAQI*

s. BANGKOK (3): THAILAND, *THAI*

t. VANCOUVER (14): CANADA, *CANADIAN*

These are just some of the places, countries and nationalities from across the world, all part of a bewildering variety representing a host of colours and creeds and cultures. They are what make this world such a fascinating place, but they are also, sadly, what so often lead to division, the differences between us leading to suspicion, hatred, war and violence.

Such divisions were there, equally, in biblical times, and in the early Church, which, in its formative days, wrestled with the question of the relationship between Jews and Gentiles – those who followed the Law of Moses and those outside it. Could non-Jews become Christians, accepted as God's people? Had the Church outgrown Judaism, or did the teaching of the Jewish Law still need to be followed?

For the Apostle Paul there was no question as to the answer. Whatever divides us is as nothing compared to what unites us. God's love is for all, not just the few. So strongly did he feel about this that he drove home his message in three separate letters. First, to the Galatians (3:28), he writes, 'There is no longer Jew or Greek, there is no longer slave or free, there is no longer male and female; for all of you are one in Christ Jesus.' Or as he put it to the Romans (10:11-13, own translation), 'As it says in scripture, "No one who puts their faith in him will be put to shame." For there is no differentiation between Jew and Greek; the same Lord is Lord of all and generous to all those who call on him. As it says again, "Everyone who calls on the name of the Lord will be saved."' Finally, there are Paul's words to the Colossians (3:11): 'There is no longer Greek and Jew, circumcised and uncircumcised, barbarian, Scythian, slave and free; but Christ is all and in all.' That doesn't, of course, do away with our differences overnight, nor does it say that we accept every view, creed or practice of those in other cultures, but it does mean that we should respect our common humanity, recognising that all are important to God, whoever they are, wherever they come from.

We live today, as people have lived throughout history, in a broken and divided world, racked by tensions and problems to which we see no easy answers. Yet it is, above all, God's world, created by and precious to him. So today we pray again for unity, for peace among nations, and for the time when it will be one world not just in name but in truth.

One World

Readings Genesis 11:1-9; John 17:1-26

Aim To illustrate the fact that we are all one in our common humanity, and that God longs for the day when the things that divide us will be overcome so that we may truly live as one.

Preparation Cut a large circle out of a piece of thick card, to represent the world. Make a hole in the centre sufficiently large for the circle to spin easily once it has been loosely but securely pinned to a board. Cut a second circle of the same size out of a thinner piece of card and cut this into twelve equal-sized segments. Colour four of these red, four blue, and four yellow. (Alternatively, you may choose to cut four segments each out of red, blue and yellow card.) In large bold letters, label the segments as follows:

AFRICA, ANTARCTICA, EUROPE, ASIA, SOUTH AMERICA, NORTH AMERICA, AUSTRALIA, EAST, WEST, NORTH, SOUTH, THIRD WORLD

Attach pieces of sticky tack to the back of these so that they can be firmly attached during the talk to the circle representing the world. Pin the latter to a board, as described above.

Talk Tell the congregation that you have some very simple questions to ask them about the world. First, how many continents are there? The answer, of course, is seven. What are these? As each is called out – Africa, Antarctica, Europe, Asia, South America, North America and Australia – stick the appropriate segment on to the circle so that one butts up against another. What two directional terms were generally used to describe the 'protagonists' in the so-called Cold War? (East and West; again, attach these segments to the circle.) Which two directions are typically used to describe the rich and poor hemispheres of the world? (North and South; once more, attach segments.) Finally, what term is often used to describe the poor and underdeveloped regions of the world? (Third World; attach the final segment.)

These various terms in different ways cover the nations and people of our planet, just as the colours we've used to represent them can be used to cover every colour in the spectrum. Ask what they are called (primary colours). What colour, for example, will blue and yellow make (green)? What will yellow and red make (orange)? What will red and blue make (purple)? And so on. But primary colours have one other fascinating and important feature, a feature which points to something equally fascinating and important about people. (Spin the circle round as fast as you can make it go. The colours will merge to make white.) The various colours go together to make a single colour; what seemed divided becomes one.

The book of Genesis paints a picture of an idealised world when all were one, in the sense that people spoke the same language, but it speaks also of the breakdown of that unity, people scattered across the earth into different nations, cultures and tongues; differences that have shown themselves in tensions and divisions across history. Such tension and division are not what God wants, as the prayer of Jesus recorded in John 17 makes plain. Having prayed for his followers and for the Church, he moves on to pray for unity in the world, for a time when all people will be united through him. That prayer reminds us that Jesus died not simply for a few but for all; that God does not just love the Church but also and equally loves the world. We share a common humanity; on that, irrespective of faith, we need to build. Today, then, we remember that, above all, this is God's world, and in that conviction we commit ourselves to, as best we can, seeking, praying for and working towards one world.

God's World

Readings   Psalm 24; John 3:13-21

Aim   To bring home that God's love and purpose extends to the whole world.

Preparation   On separate strips of paper/card, print the following in large bold letters:

> JAPAN, EUROPE, SOUTH AMERICA, UNITED STATES, SOUTH AFRICA, SWEDEN, AUSTRALIA, INDIA, DENMARK, ISRAEL, AFRICA, MEXICO, TURKEY, HONG KONG, EGYPT, LAPLAND, ICELAND, GERMANY, HOLLAND, THAILAND, OSLO, FRANCE, TANZANIA, HUNGARY, ETHIOPIA, WEST INDIES, OMAN, RUSSIA, LIECHTENSTEIN, DOMINICAN REPUBLIC

Attach sticky tack or magnetic tape to the back of each and retain in the order printed, ready for use later in the talk. For the clues marked 'Shape' below, trace the shape of the country or continent in question on to a piece of coloured card and then cut this out, ready to display during the talk as a clue.

Talk   Tell the congregation that, in keeping with One World Sunday, you have prepared a geographical quiz. Most of the answers are countries or continents; a few relate to provinces, principalities, capital cities and such like. As each correct answer is given, stick the matching word on to a display board, using one to two columns as necessary, as shown beneath the quiz clues below:

1. The capital of this country is Tokyo (JAPAN)

2. France, Holland and the UK are all part of this continent (EUROPE)

3. Shape: (SOUTH AMERICA)

4. George Washington was once President of this country (UNITED STATES)

5. A country that was formerly separated by apartheid (SOUTH AFRICA)

6. The home country of Sven Goran Eriksson (SWEDEN)

7. Shape: (AUSTRALIA)

8. The Taj Mahal can be found here (INDIA)

9. A place perhaps where you might expect to find a Great Dane? (DENMARK)

10. A country in which most of Old Testament is set (ISRAEL)

11. Shape: (AFRICA)

12. A country in Central America where people wear sombreros (MEXICO)

13. A country which sounds like a bird eaten at Christmas (TURKEY)

14. A province handed back to China in 1997 (HONG KONG)

15. Land of the Pharaohs (EGYPT)

16. Reputedly the home of Father Christmas (LAPLAND)

17. This sounds like a very cold country (ICELAND)

18. This country used to be divided by the Berlin Wall (GERMANY)

19. A flat country famous for its tulips and dykes (HOLLAND)

20. Bangkok is the capital of this country (THAILAND)

21. The capital of Norway (OSLO)

22. The nearest Continental country to England (FRANCE)

23. Mount Kilimanjaro is on this country's border with Kenya (TANZANIA)

24. A country that sounds in need of food (HUNGARY)

25. An African country plagued by famine (ETHIOPIA)

26. Another name for the Caribbean, this region is famed for its Test Cricket teams (WEST INDIES)

27. An oil-producing country in the Middle East (OMAN)

28. A country that used to be at the heart of the old Soviet Union (RUSSIA)

29. A tiny principality in central Europe (LIECHTENSTEIN)

30. A country in the Caribbean, famed for its production of coffee, cocoa and bananas (DOMINICAN REPUBLIC)

JAPAN
EUROPE
SOUTH AMERICA
UNITED STATES
SOUTH AFRICA

SWEDEN
AUSTRALIA
INDIA
DENMARK

ISRAEL

AFRICA
MEXICO

TURKEY
HONG KONG
EGYPT

LAPLAND
ICELAND
GERMANY
HOLLAND
THAILAND

OSLO
FRANCE

TANZANIA
HUNGARY
ETHIOPIA

WEST INDIES
OMAN
RUSSIA
LIECHTENSTEIN
DOMINICAN REPUBLIC

These are just some of the numerous countries and places in our world, together representing an astonishing variety of creeds, colours, cultures and customs. They remind us that our own country is but one tiny part of the wider world, a world that is all important and precious to God, part of his plans. Ask if anyone can see evidence of that truth hidden in our list of countries, i.e. 'Jesus said, "I am the light of the world"' (John 8:12), spelt out by reading the first letter of each word.

God wants us to remember that just as all people are his concern so they are ours to. We have a responsibility to other nations, in terms of economic and environmental issues, as well as in our prayers and in supporting the work of mission. We have something to give but also something to receive, each of us being part of the family of humankind. Thank God for our world, but above all, never forget that it is *his* world first.

All Saints' Day

Keeping Going

Readings 1 Corinthians 9:24-27; Hebrews 12:1-2

Aim Through the example of those who have kept the faith, to point to the importance of perseverance in discipleship.

Preparation For this talk you will need two wind-up or battery-powered novelty figures (available from gift boutiques, toy shops and so forth), the sort that waddle along on two legs. One of these needs to be fairly fast but tall and unstable, the other needs to be a little slower but short and squat, and thus more stable over uneven ground. For the purposes of description, I will refer to these as Figures A and B, but you may like to invent names for them, depending on the toys you choose. You will also need a long table or board for the toys to race on and a large thick cloth with which to cover the board / table for a later race.

Talk Show the congregation your two toys and tell them that you are going to race them against each other. Take a show of hands as to who they think will win. Barring an unforeseen catastrophe, the taller and faster toy should win easily. Rerun the race a couple of times to show that this result was no fluke. Now spread the cloth over the table, rumpling it up to produce a slightly uneven surface, not sufficient to interrupt the progress of Figure B but enough to make Figure A topple over. Ask the congregation once more who they think will win, and then demonstrate. Again, rerun the race a couple of times to prove the result was no accident.

As long as the going is smooth, Figure A wins easily, but when it gets rough then Figure A comes unstuck and Figure B comes through to win, the only one able to complete the course. This calls to mind the words of a song from a film a few years back: 'When the going gets tough . . . the tough get going.' And that's exactly the message in our readings today, two passages that remind us the going isn't always easy when it comes to following Jesus. 'They were stoned to death,' says the book of Hebrews, 'they were sawn in two, they were killed by the sword; they went about in skins of sheep and goats, destitute, persecuted, tormented' (Hebrews 11:37). Thankfully, we today do not face such dangers for being Christians but it is still not always easy in a world where few have any time for the gospel, where life doesn't always go as we hope, and where we will encounter our fair share of difficulties and disappointments. It's easy to call ourselves Christians and to make an impulsive commitment, but will we be able to keep faith through thick and thin? If we are to do so we need to work at our faith and nurture our relationship with Christ. In the words of Paul, 'Do you not know that in a race the runners all compete, but only one receives the prize? Run in such a way that you may win it' (1 Corinthians 9:24). Or as the writer to the Hebrews puts it, 'Let us also lay aside every weight and the sin that clings so closely, and let us run with perseverance the race that is set before us, looking to Jesus the pioneer and perfecter of our faith' (Hebrews 12:1b-2a).

All Saints Together

Readings   1 Corinthians 1:1-3; Ephesians 2:11-22

Aim   To show that though we revere some especially as saints, in God's eyes we are all saints simply by being part of the Church.

Preparation   On separate strips of coloured card, print the following:

> PARROTS, LIONS, GOLDFINCHES, BEES,
> KITTENS, BISHOPS, GEESE, PIPERS,
> ACROBATS, SHIPS, WOLVES, CROWS,
> FISH, DUCKS, LARKS, CATTLE, SHEEP

Affix magnetic tape or sticky tack to the back of each, and arrange on a board as shown below:

```
P A R R O T S
        L I O N S
                G O L D F I N C H E S
            B E E
        K I T T E N S
        B I S H O P S
            G E E S E
    P I P E R S
A C R O B A T S
            S H I P S
    W O L V E S
            C R O W S
        F I S H
            D U C K S
        L A R K S
            C A T T L E
        S H E E P
```

On strips of card of a different colour, print the following:

> GAGGLE, HERD, CHARM, SWARM, MURDER,
> PRIDE, SKIRL, LITTER, PADDLING, SHOAL,
> BENCH, PACK, PANDEMONIUM, ARMADA,
> FLOCK, TROUPE, EXALTATION

Affix magnetic tape or sticky tack to the back of each, and retain for use later in the talk, ideally for display on a second board.

Talk Ask the congregation what we might call a collection or group of questions. Several answers could be given, such as 'an exam' or 'a test', but the one you are looking for is 'a quiz'. Explain that you have a quiz today concerned with the various groups of people, animals or objects listed on the board, some very easy, some very hard. Ask the following questions (point to the appropriate entry on the first board as you do so), and as each correct answer is given, display it on a second whiteboard, as shown after the quiz questions:

1. What do we call a group of wolves? *A PACK*
2. What do we call a group of pipers? *A SKIRL*
3. What do we call a group of ducks? *A PADDLING*
4. What do we call a group of fish? *A SHOAL*
5. What do we call a group of ships? *AN ARMARDA*
6. What do we call a group of lions? *A PRIDE*
7. What do we call a group of parrots?
   A PANDEMONIUM
8. What do we call a group of larks?
   AN EXALTATION
9. What do we call a group of bees? *A SWARM*
10. What do we call a group of kittens? *A LITTER*
11. What do we call a group of sheep? *A FLOCK*
12. What do we call a group of geese? *A GAGGLE*
13. What do we call a group of crows? *A MURDER*
14. What do we call a group of acrobats? *A TROUPE*
15. What do we call a group of cattle? *A HERD*
16. What do we call a group of bishops? *A BENCH*
17. What do we call a group of goldfinches?
    A CHARM

```
        P A C K
  S K I R L
P A D D L I N G
        S H O A L
    A R M A D A
      P R I D E
      P A N D E M O N I U M
E X A L T A T I O N
        S W A R M
    L I T T E R
    F L O C K
        G A G G L E
M U R D E R
        T R O U P E
        H E R D
      B E N C H
  C H A R M
```

Without commenting yet on the arrangement of questions and answers, ask what we call a collection of Christians. The answer you are looking for is 'a church'. Ask what we call a collection of churches. The answer you are looking for this time is '*the* Church'. There is, however, another answer we could give to both those questions. Ask if anyone can think what word we might use to cover both a collection of Christians and a collection of churches. The answer is 'saints'. We tend to use the term for a select few, those who have shown special faith or holiness in their lives, but in the original Greek of the New Testament it is applied to all those who love and follow Jesus. So Paul starts the first of his letters to the Corinthians (1:2): 'To the church of God that is in Corinth, to those who are sanctified in Christ, called to be saints, together with all those who in every place call on the name of our Lord Jesus Christ, both their Lord and ours.' Or as he wrote similarly to the Ephesians (2:19): 'You are, therefore, no longer strangers and aliens, but fellow-citizens with the saints and members of God's family.' Those words apply not just to then but to now, not simply to those Paul was writing to in Corinth and Ephesus, but to all who have committed their lives to Christ. We are part of the family of God's people in every age, and those who will share in the inheritance of his eternal kingdom. The answer is there in the questions and answers of our quiz. Ask if anyone can see the two hidden messages – TOGETHER THE CHURCH and ALL SAINTS TOGETHER. In other words, we are all different, just like the various groups we've looked at – each reflecting a unique blend of background, temperament and circumstances that has made us what we are – but as Christians, we are not only TOGETHER THE CHURCH but also, by God's grace, ALL SAINTS TOGETHER.

Remembrance
Sunday

Let's Grow Feet!

Readings Deuteronomy 6:4-9; Luke 22:14-23

Aim To emphasise the importance of remembering those who gave their lives in the two World Wars and subsequent conflicts, and to illustrate how Remembrance Sunday and Remembrance Day help us do just that.

Preparation On separate squares of card, one per letter, print the following, in large bold letters:

L G F E R E T O E S W T

Fasten sticky tack or magnetic tape to the front and back of each letter, and retain for use during the talk.

Talk Tell the congregation that you want to test their memory today. Hold up the lettered 'cards' you have prepared and announce that you want people to remember where you put them. Place the cards, face down, on a whiteboard, as below, announcing each letter as you do so, starting at the bottom right-hand corner and working upwards so as not to give the game away (the letter is shown in outline on each square, though of course this will not be seen by the congregation):

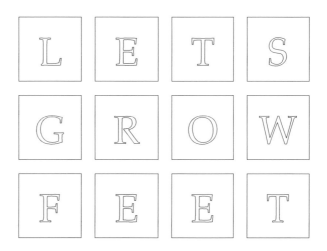

Ask if anyone can tell you where an O is. How about a G, an F, an E, an S and so forth (the chances are that very few people will guess correctly). Continue until you feel the congregation have had enough. Now announce that you are going to make things a lot easier. Carefully reposition the letters, face downwards, so that they again spell out the message LETS / GROW / FEET, but this time tell the congregation what you have done. Ask if someone can find you the letter O now, and so on (turn over each letter as it is correctly identified). The congregation should have no problem in matching every letter on the board.

Remembering isn't always easy. With the best will in the world, we can forget even important things. That's why we invent tools, like knots in a hankie, memo boards and mnemonics to help us remember, and that, of course, is what we've done in our puzzle today. Not that there's much point in remembering the words LETS GROW FEET, unless we're playing a memory game, but the letters can easily be rearranged into an infinitely more important message. Arrange the letters on the whiteboard, as follows:

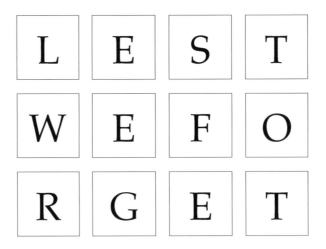

The message now is clear enough: words central to this day and to Remembrance Day itself. Many will be wearing poppies, some will listen to the sounding of the Last Post or the firing of a salute, some will repeat the words 'We will remember them' after the equally familiar lines 'They shall not grow old, as we that are left grow old. Age shall not weary them, nor the years condemn. At the going down of the sun and in the morning, we will remember them.'

Why do we do such things? Simply, but vitally, to remember those who gave their lives for us, and those who continue to give their lives in the armed forces today. We do this, lest we forget; because the lessons of the past are too important to be forgotten.

It is many years now since the last World War ended, and there are fewer and fewer people old enough to remember first-hand what happened. But, just as the Jews were told in the book of Deuteronomy to bind the words of the Law as an emblem to their foreheads and write them on the doorposts of their houses, so we need to remember the cost of war and the price of peace, LEST WE FORGET.

Remembering and Learning

Readings Various readings are included as part of this talk.

Aim This talk, like the last one, uses the idea of a memory game, but this time the emphasis is on learning from what's gone before; an idea which is subsequently expanded in terms of learning what God has done for us and from the sacrifice of those who have given their lives in war.

Preparation On separate squares of card, one per letter, print two sets of the following, in large bold letters:

T I T N O D T E R G O F

Fasten sticky tack or magnetic tape to the *front and back* of each letter, and arrange these face down on a whiteboard, as follows (the letter is shown in outline on each square, though of course this will not be seen by the participants):

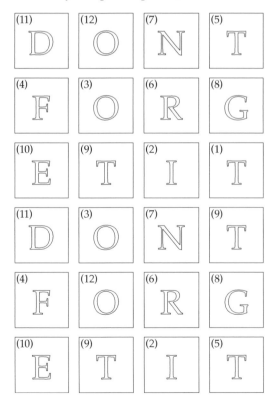

Next, on separate slips of paper but in normal print size, print off the following Bible verses:

(1) Deuteronomy 4:9a: 'But take care and watch yourselves closely, so as neither to forget the things that your eyes have seen nor to let them slip from your mind all the days of your life.'

(2) Deuteronomy 4:23a: 'So be careful not to forget the covenant that the Lord your God made with you.'

(3) Deuteronomy 8:11a: 'Take care that you do not forget the Lord your God, by failing to keep his commandments, his ordinances, and his statutes.'

(4) Psalm 103:2: 'Bless the Lord, O my soul, and do not forget all his benefits.'

(5) Psalm 106:10, 13a, 21: 'So he saved them from the hand of the foe, and delivered them from the hand of the enemy . . . But they soon forgot his works . . . They forgot God, their Saviour, who had done great things for them in Egypt.'

(6) Psalm 119:83b, 93, 109b: 'I have not forgotten your statutes . . . I will never forget your precepts, for by them you have given me life . . . I do not forget your law.'

(7) Proverbs 4:5: 'Get wisdom; get insight: do not forget, nor turn away.'

(8) Proverbs 3:1: 'My child, do not forget my teaching, but let your heart keep my commandments.'

(9) Jeremiah 3:21: 'A voice on the bare heights is heard, the plaintive weeping of Israel's children, because they have perverted their way, they have forgotten the Lord their God.'

(10) James 1:25: 'But those who look into the perfect law . . . being not hearers who forget but doers who act – they will be blessed in their doing.'

(11) Jeremiah 2:32b: 'Yet my people have forgotten me, days without number.'

(12) Isaiah 51:13a: 'You have forgotten the Lord your Maker, who stretched out the heavens and laid the foundations of the earth.'

Distribute these to members of the congregation prior to the talk/service, making sure that they know which number reading theirs is, and prime them to read the verse when the corresponding pair of numbers comes up during the talk.

Talk Tell the congregation that you have prepared a memory game and ask for three volunteers to take part. The aim of the game is very simple: in two guesses to find two letters that match. However, since there are more than two of some letters, each square has also been numbered, participants need to find letters for which the numbers also match. When a matching pair is found, place these face upwards on the board in the same positions from which they were taken, and ask whoever has the reading with corresponding number to stand up and read his or her verse (it may be as well to repeat the verse afterwards, for the benefit of those who are hard of hearing). Continue until all the letters on the board have been overturned.

The game is fairly straightforward, but it has an important lesson, which of course we can see spelt out now and repeated on the board: DON'T FORGET IT! We need to learn from what has happened if we hope to get things right next time. That is the message equally in each of our Bible verses: remember what God has done, is the constant refrain, often addressed to those who have failed to do that, forgetting his love and turning their backs on his will.

The message, of course, is hugely appropriate for Remembrance Sunday and Remembrance Day itself. We look back and remember not simply for the sake of it, but with a view to learning the lessons of the past, so that if possible peace can be preserved but if necessary evil is confronted before it is allowed to get out of hand. Don't forget all you owe to God; don't forget all you owe to others: remember, learn and apply the lessons for today.

Church
Anniversary

Building Bricks

Readings   Ephesians 2:1-22; 1 Peter 2:1-10

Aim   To stress that the health and future of any church depends on how far its life and witness are based on Christ.

Preparation   For this talk, you will need 12 small plastic flowerpots, a pack of playing cards, and nine household bricks with which to build a mini-church building. Construct a 'building' out of playing cards by laying them edge up against each other, laying cards flat on top of these, and subsequently adding other 'storeys' of cards. The resulting edifice will be very unstable, so take care not to disturb it and be prepared, if necessary, to rebuild it swiftly.

Arrange the flowerpots into a 'pyramid wall', five pots in a row at the base, four pots balanced on these, and three more balanced on these. Finally, attach a large sticky label to each brick, turning five on end, and label them as illustrated below.

PEACE	SERVICE

FELLOWSHIP	WORSHIP

CHRIST	FAITH	HOPE	GRACE	PRAYER

Stack the bricks into a wall comprising three rows of three, with the words facing away from the congregation (again, see next page). If you erect the wall on a communion table, be sure to cover this first with a thick blanket to prevent any damage.

Talk Ask how many people remember the story of 'The Three Little Pigs', and then ask if anyone can remember what happens in the story. Tell the congregation that with their help you're going to re-enact that story in your talk, and ask for three volunteers to have a go at blowing your walls down.

Invite your first volunteer to blow down the playing-card building. It should collapse almost immediately. Invite your second volunteer to blow down the flowerpot wall. This will probably collapse as easily as the first. Ask your final volunteer to blow down the brick wall. They will, of course, have no chance whatsoever!

The reason, obviously, is that, unlike the playing cards and flowerpots, the bricks are strong and heavy, built to last. And there's a lesson in all this concerning the Church. For a church to last and be strong, it needs to be built of the right materials; not bricks, but other equally important building blocks. Turn the bricks round, reconstructing them so that the labels face the congregation, as follows:

PRAYER	GRACE			
CHRIST	FAITH	FELLOWSHIP	SERVICE	HOPE
		WORSHIP	PEACE	

These are the building blocks of the Church, whether this or any other fellowship. The cornerstone, of course, is *Christ*. Alongside this we need *faith*, a faith that shows itself both in *prayer* and *worship* and also in service. We need time to share *fellowship*, living in *peace* with one another. We need to be a people of *hope*, trusting in what God is doing and is going to do among us, and confident also of his eternal purpose for us and all his people. We cannot, though, make all that happen ourselves; we depend finally on his *grace* to take and shape us into the church he wants us to be.

You may be wondering about one final thing. What binds these building blocks together? With real bricks, of course, we'd use cement, but with the Church, it's different: the final thing needed is love. We are here today to celebrate another chapter in the life of this church, and to look forward to what we hope will be many more chapters to come. How many there will be, and what will be written in them, depends on how far these things are part of our life together; how far these are the building blocks through which Christ can continue to build his church here in this place.

What the Church Can Become

Readings   John 17:20-23; Ephesians 2:11-22

Aim   To explore what, by God's grace, the Church is (or should be) always in the process of becoming.

Preparation   Print (to scale and in as large letters as possible) the following letters:

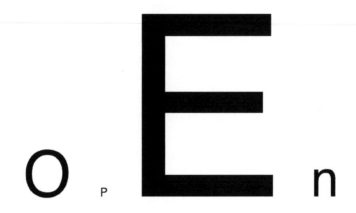

Fasten magnetic tape or sticky tack to the back of each, and arrange the letters as on the next page.

Talk Point to the 'picture' you have prepared and ask what it represents. The congregation will rightly observe that it portrays a church. Agree, but remind them of the often-repeated saying that the Church is the people, not the building. Proceed to illustrate that by separating the letters into the following four words:

OPEN
CARING
UNITED
CHURCH

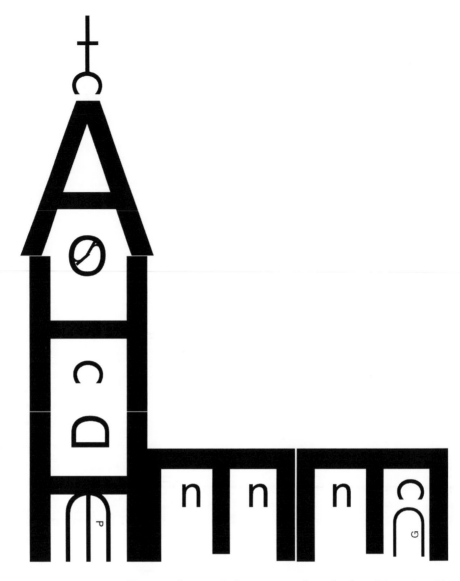

Here is the goal that every church should set itself: of being an open, caring and united church – open to all, whoever they may be; caring for all within the fellowship; and united in faith and vision, both in terms of the immediate family and the wider family of the Church. We never, of course, reach perfection, and often fall well short of that ideal, but as we come today to celebrate another year in the life of this fellowship, let us consider what God is constantly striving to help us become, and so commit ourselves to being more truly the church he would have us be.

Names from the Past

Reading   Hebrews 13:7-8

Aim   This talk – suitable only for those churches that have commemoratory plaques around the church or items such as tables, books, chairs dedicated to individuals – emphasises the debt we owe to the past and the fact that we have a responsibility to present and future generations.

Preparation   The only preparation needed for this talk is to look round the various plaques/dedications within your church and to prepare a list of questions concerning these – for example: Who died in [year]? Who gave the [item/s] to this church and in memory of whom? Who served as [position] in this church from [dates]? Who founded this church? Tailor the questions to reflect the wording of dedications, so as to give clues to the identity of each individual.

Talk   Tell the congregation that since they are celebrating an anniversary, you have prepared a quiz concerning the past history of the church. Ask the various questions you have prepared.

All of these people – some known personally to us, some just names – represent those who have been part of this church, serving God in their own different ways within it. They are part of the story of this fellowship, part of *our* story. We tread in their footsteps, carrying on the work they were part of, and if we would truly honour their names, then we will do our utmost to take forward the life and witness of this church so that future generations may be part of its story in turn. We may not have plaques or memorials erected to remember us, but out legacy will be having helped build for the future in the service of Christ, the same yesterday, today and tomorrow.

Music/Songs of Praise Service

Make Music in Your Hearts

Readings   Psalm 98; Colossians 3:16-17

Aim   To affirm the place of music and song in worship.

Preparation   On separate strips of card / paper, print the following in large bold letters:

> MUSICAL INSTRUMENT, MUSICAL CHAIRS,
> SONGS OF PRAISE, GOING FOR A SONG,
> MUSIC SYSTEM, FOLKSONG,
> MUSIC FESTIVAL, SONG THRUSH,
> THEME MUSIC, PLAINSONG, MUSICAL BOX,
> ROCK MUSIC, THE SOUND OF MUSIC,
> MUSICIAN, ORGAN MUSIC, EVENSONG,
> WATER MUSIC, SWAN SONG, ANNIE'S SONG,
> EUROVISION SONG CONTEST,
> SING A SONG OF SIXPENCE

Fix sticky tack to the back of each, ready for use later in the talk. Print the same words again and arrange on a board as follows:

```
    R O C K  M U S I C
         O R G A N  M U S I C
       F O L K S O N G
  M U S I C  F E S T I V A L
               M U S I C A L  C H A I R S
     T H E  S O U N D  O F  M U S I C
       E V E N S O N G
       P L A I N S O N G
     M U S I C A L  I N S T R U M E N T
     M U S I C I A N
S I N G  A  S O N G  O F  S I X P E N C E
M U S I C  S Y S T E M
E U R O V I S I O N  S O N G  C O N T E S T
          M U S I C A L  B O X
  G O I N G  F O R  A  S O N G
              T H E M E  M U S I C
     A N N I E S  S O N G
         S W A N  S O N G
     W A T E R  M U S I C
   S O N G  T H R U S H
     S O N G S  O F  P R A I S E
```

Turn this side of the board away from the congregation, to be revealed at the end of the talk, and use the other side for the quiz as below.

Talk Tell the congregation that in keeping with a music and songs of praise service, you have prepared a quiz for them on a musical theme. All the answers have the word 'music' or 'song', or variants of these, in them. Read out the clues below, one by one, and as the correct answer is given stick it on to the board, arranging them as displayed on the next page:

- We make music on this: *Musical instrument*

- A traditional, boisterous and well-loved party game: *Musical chairs*

- The name of a long-running religious TV programme: *Songs of Praise*

- Being sold cheap, or the name of a once-popular TV programme on antiques: *Going for a Song*

- Another name for a hi-fi: *Music system*

- Another name for a traditional country song: *Folksong*

- A major event, held annually in such places as Cheltenham: *Music Festival*

- Like the blackbird and nightingale, this bird is celebrated for its song: *Song thrush*

- Music used at the start and end of a films and TV programmes: *Theme music*

- The name given to the chanting of monks: *Plainsong*

- A child's plaything: *Musical box*

- Heavy metal is an example of this: *Rock music*

- A film shown just about every Christmas! *The Sound of Music*

- The name we give to anyone who makes music: *Musician*

- The sort of music most often associated with church: *Organ music*

- A traditional church service in which the choir play a key role: *Evensong*

- A famous work by Handel that we might sing in the bath! *Water Music*

- The last performance of a celebrity: *Swan song*

- A John Denver song later played by the flautist James Galway: *Annie's Song*

- An international song competition held each year: *Eurovision Song Contest*

- The nursery rhyme that ends with a blackbird pecking off a nose: *Sing a Song of Sixpence*

M U S I C A L   I N S T R U M E N T
M U S I C A L   C H A I R S
S O N G S   O F   P R A I S E
G O I N G   F O R   A   S O N G
M U S I C   S Y S T E M
F O L K S O N G
M U S I C   F E S T I V A L
S O N G   T H R U S H
T H E M E   M U S I C
P L A I N S O N G
M U S I C A L   B O X
R O C K   M U S I C
T H E   S O U N D   O F   M U S I C
M U S I C I A N
O R G A N   M U S I C
E V E N S O N G
W A T E R   M U S I C
S W A N   S O N G
A N N I E S   S O N G
E U R O V I S I O N   S O N G   C O N T E S T
S I N G   A   S O N G   O F   S I X P E N C E

We can express ourselves through music in innumerable ways, just as there are an incalculable number of hymns, songs, melodies and tunes that we could have sung, played or listened to during this service. But we are not here simply to enjoy a good sing or tune, pleasurable enough though that might be. We are here for a reason: a reason that the various answers we've given tonight make clear.

Ask if anyone can see the first message hidden in the answers, and then read this through again yourself. 'Sing to the Lord a new song': that's why we're here, the motivation behind our songs and music today. That's why the hymns, songs and choruses we've shared were written, each designed to be offered to God in worship.

Turn over the board and reveal the second arrangement of words, and again ask if anyone can see the hidden message. 'Make music in your hearts': that's the second important ingredient of this service. We're not simply going through the motions, or at least we shouldn't be. What we sing should be offered from the heart; the music we make should be an expression of praise offered in thanksgiving and adoration. God has given us the gift of music, and we thank him *for* it; but, equally important, we thank him *through* it.

Sing to the Lord a New Song

Readings Psalm 96:1-9; Ephesians 5:15-20

Aim To emphasise the importance of joyfully, spontaneously and faithfully giving praise and worship to God.

Preparation Borrow CD recordings of recent chart hits from young people in your church, family or circle of friends, ensuring, if possible, that these are the most recent releases of each artist. Have these ready in the service to play a brief excerpt from each.

Talk Ask how many of the young people like music. Who is their favourite group or singer and what is their favourite song? Tell the congregation that you have a pop quiz for them: all they have to do is listen to the snatches of music you are going to play and identify the name of the artist and song, and, if possible, give some idea of when the song was first released and what position it made in the charts. Play snippets from the CDs.

Some of you may harbour secret dreams of one day being popstars, but few people have what it takes to make it to the top. Yet there is one sense in which we are all called not only to sing, but also, like the artists we've heard today, to constantly bring out new songs – and that sense is spelt out for us in the opening words of Psalm 96: 'O sing to the Lord a new song; sing to the Lord, all the earth. Sing to the Lord, bless his name; tell of his salvation from day to day' (vv. 1-2). Each one of us is called to offer worship to God, joyfully and sincerely to sing his praise; not as a duty but as a privilege, not as an obligation but as something we simply cannot help but do. Whether it is a hymn of praise or simply our hearts singing within us does not matter; what counts is that we want to respond in adoration and glad thanksgiving to the one who alone is worthy of all glory and honour, praise and worship.